DINOBIBI

JAPAN

TRAVEL FOR KIDS

CONTENTS

KYOTO

OSAKA

Culture and Traditions (pg. 25)

Native Planst & Animals (pg. 34)

Famous People (pg. 38)

Major Cities & Attractions (pg. 42)

Hello everyone!

I am so excited and happy to invite you to my country, the beautiful and lovely Japan. My name is Hinata. I am a 10-year-old girl living in Tokyo with my parents. I will be your companion right through your journey across the different parts of my wonderful country.

Before I tell you more about myself, I would like to know more about you.
Can you please complete this little questionnaire for me?

Your name:

Which country are you from:

Who are you traveling with?

Which places in Japan are you most exicited about? Why?

Now, let me tell you about myself. As you already know, I am Hinata. My mother, Hina Sato, teaches English in a school close to where we live. My father, Akira Sato, is a computer engineer working for a big Japanese company. I am an only child.

In my country, going to school is seen as very important, and my parents keep reminding me about the importance of learning as much as I can in school. But, no one complains about going to school in my country because of many reasons.

Can you guess what the capital of Japan is?

1. Osaka
2. Tokyo
3. Kyoto

(Answer – 2. Tokyo)

Teachers are not allowed to send children out of the class. There is a law against this in my country, which even applies to misbehaving students. The teacher will have to find other ways to manage misbehaving kids. I think my mother's high level of patience comes from having to remain calm and cool even when her students create a ruckus in class!

We wear school uniforms and we even have indoor footwears as we're required to take off our shoes when coming in to school.

The public schools in Japan serve the same meal to all the students. We have no choice but to finish what's on our plate. In my class (like in all other classes), we take turns serving meals to our classmates. We eat our meals in the classroom along with our teachers who also get the same meal.

Also, we don't have cleaners and janitors in our school. The students are responsible for cleaning the classrooms, the cafeteria, and the toilets too! But, we don't work alone; our teachers and even our principal join in every day to help us keep our school spic-and-span!

The best part about schooling in Japan is that we are not allowed to be failed in any grade. No matter how well or poorly we do on our tests and assignments, all of us get a school-completion certificate. But, our test scores matter a lot when we apply for college admissions. So, even if we don't have to work hard to complete school, we have to work hard if we want to get into a good college.

Now, that I have told you some really interesting facts about my school, let me share more interesting things about my beautiful country, Japan. Japan has a lot of other names including Nippon, Yamato, and Wa.

Japan has been called 'The Land of the Rising Sun' since ancient times, when the Chinese would see the sun rising in the direction where Japan archipelago is. The name "Nippon" meaning, "Origin of the Sun" is believed to be coined by Prince Shotoku in 600 AD.

Fun Facts:

There are about 127 million people living in Japan today.

Japanese is the spoken language in my country.

Majority of the people in my country follow Shintoism and Buddhism.

Japan is a chain of islands lying on the eastern coast of Asia. The Sea of Japan is located between my country and the main part of Asia. But, we are part of Asia.

There are four main islands including Hokkaido, Honshu, Shikoku, and Kyushu.

Other than the four main islands maintained, Japan has nearly 4000 smaller islands or isles. The islands of Japan extend from Russia's north coast (in the north) to the South East China Sea (in the south).

SEA OF JAPAN

AKITA

TOKYO

KYOTO

OSAKA

EAST CHINA SEA

NORTH PACIFIC OCEAN

Japan is also located on the Pacific 'Ring of Fire' which is a chain of volcanoes that are responsible for the most powerful tsunamis and volcanic eruptions in the past few years!

A volcanic eruption takes place when hot materials from deep under the earth are thrown out onto the surface of the earth!

Tsunamis (huge sea or ocean waves) are caused when there is an earthquake or any other disturbance in the sea or ocean. Some volcanic eruptions and tsunamis can cause a lot of damage and destruction.

Japan has over 100 active volcanoes. Over 1000 earthquakes happen in my country every year. Thankfully, not all of them are dangerous.

Japan does not have any land borders with other countries. Remember, it is made up of many islands. But, Japan shares maritime borders with other countries including the Philippines, South Korea, Russia, China and North Korea.

Japanese people take nature very seriously. We have a deep affection for Mother Nature. Shintoism is one of the oldest religions of the world and is still very popular in my country.

Shintoism teaches us that natural geographical features like forests, waterfalls, mountains, rivers, and others have a spirit of their own. So, we consider all elements of nature as sacred.

Pop Quiz!

Can you guess what was Japan's capital just before Tokyo?

1. Kyoto
2. Osaka
3. Yokohama

(Answer — 1. Kyoto)

What do you think is the Japanese name of Japan?

1. Nippon
2. Japan
3. Japon

(Answer — 1. Nippon)

What is the name of the highest mountain peak in Japan?
(Hint: It's also a volcano!)

1. Mount Fuji
2. Mount Takao
3. Mount Haku

(Answer — 1. Mount Fuji; the last time this volcano erupted was in 1707. Since then, it is sleeping). More about Mount Fuji later on.

Important Rivers and Lakes of Japan

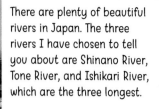

There are plenty of beautiful rivers in Japan. The three rivers I have chosen to tell you about are Shinano River, Tone River, and Ishikari River, which are the three longest.

Shinano River

This is the longest and widest river in Japan. It rises in the Japanese Alps in the Honshu Island. Its starting point is Mount Kobushi and flows in an almost northeasterly direction and enters the sea of Japan at a place called Niigata. This river is 367 km (267 miles) long, and is known as Chikuma River in its upper reaches.

Tone River

Starting on the Omnikami Mountains in Gunma Prefecture, this river empties into the Pacific Ocean at Choshi. Its length is 322 km (about 200 miles).

The Tone River was once a raging river with its waters rushing wildly along its path. However, a lot of towns, cities, and castles were built along its shores which reduced the speed of the river.

Ishikari River

The Ishikari River is 268 km (about 167 miles) long, starting in the middle of the Kitami Mountains on the Hokkaido Island and emptying into the Sea of Japan at the Ishikari Bay. The name Ishikari comes from the Ainu word, ishikaribetsu, which translates to 'greatly meandering river.' The Ainu is an indigenous (original inhabitants) group of people living in Hokkaido. The Ishikari River is very sacred to the Ainu people.

Lakes of Japan

Let me tell you about three of my favorite lakes in Japan. They are Biwa, Kawaguchi, and Kasumigaura. Lakes occupy only 1% of the land area in my country.

Lake Kawaguchi — This lake is one of the Fuji Five Lakes that surrounds Mount Fuji. This lake is the base for many people who want to climb Mount Fuji. You can get the best view of Mount Fuji from the shores of Lake Kawaguchi.

Lake Biwa — Located in Shiga Prefecture, Lake Biwa is the largest lake in Japan, is one of the 20 oldest lakes in the world, and was formed more than 4 million years ago. It covers an area of 672 square kilometers (about 260 square miles) and is fed by more than 460 streams from the surrounding mountains. It was one of the most important inland routes carrying rice and other goods from north Japan to Kyoto and Osaka in south Japan. The pearl cultivation industry used to thrive here, and Biwa pearls became world famous. Today, sadly, this industry is not doing as well.

There are many beautiful beaches on the lakeshore. You can also find hot springs, lush green parks, and hiking paths all around Lake Biwa. A 220-km (a little over 136 miles) cycling track can be found here. It is one of the most beautiful cycling routes in Japan where you can see some great views of the lake and the mountains around it. Of course, we kids cannot think of cycling there. Maybe you could keep it on your wishlist. When you return to Japan as an adult, we could try it!

Lake Kasumigaura — This is the second largest lake in Japan after Lake Biwa, and is located 60 km (about 37 miles) north-east of Tokyo. You can see some stunning views of Mt. Tsukuba from Lake Kasumi-gaura.

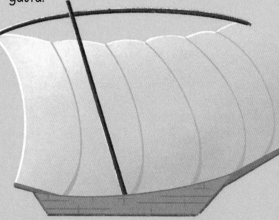

From July to October, we can ride on the hobikibune fishing boats which have huge sails. Riding on these beautiful boats is thrilling.

Mountains of Japan

Mount Fuji is the most easily recognizable peak of Japan. It is the highest mountain peak in Japan and rises 3776 m (or 12389 ft).

Mount Fuji actually consists of three different volcanoes stacked one over the other. The bottom-most volcano is Komitake, the second layer is Kofuji, and the youngest and the topmost volcano is Fuji!

There are five lakes (collectively called Fuji Five Lakes) around this spectacular peak. The names of these five lakes are Yamanakako, Kawaguchi (yes, we discussed this lake under 'Lakes of Japan), Motosuko, Saiko, and Shojiko.

The Japanese Alps run right down the center of the largest island, Honshu. More than 70% of Japan is covered with mountains. The mountains and rivers together result in some spectacular waterfalls.

By the way, there are 'three holy mountains' in Japan that are considered sacred by the people of Japan. They are Mount Fuji, Mount Tate, and Mount Haku. Mount Fuji has a symmetrical shape which is quite rare for a volcano.

When was the last eruption of Mount Fuji?

1. 1950
2. 2000
3. 1707

(Answer: Year 1707! The volcano erupted on December 16, 1707, and is believed to have continued until New Year's Day, 1708!)

Did you know that Hagoromo Falls is called 'The Niagara Falls of the East?' In case you don't know, Niagara Falls is one of the most beautiful waterfalls in the world lying on the border between the USA and Canada.

Flag of Japan

A small note about the 'red' color of the color; it is not red but 'crimson.' Crimson is a deeper red than the normal red.

The Japanese flag is also called Hinomaru (sun disc) or Nisshoki (sun-mark flag).

It is one of the simplest ones to draw with just a big red dot right in the middle of a white rectangle.

The flag was in use from 701 and is documented in Shoku Nihongi, an old Japanese classic history book. But, the flag wasn't adopted officially until 1999!
The reason why the sun is such an important symbol for us Japanese is we believe the sun-goddess Amaterasu founded and established Japan more than 2700 years ago.

Japan is also called the 'Land of the Rising Sun' because of this belief that the sun goddess is the ancestor of the Japanese emperor which is why he is also referred to as the 'son of the sun.'

Pop Quiz!

So, now you know that the red, oops, crimson color represents the sun. Do you know what the white color background represents?

1. Peace
2. Harmony
3. Integrity and honesty of the Japanese people

(Answer: (3) Integrity and honesty of the Japanese people)

What is the red circle in the Japanese flag symbolize?

1. Just a red dot
2. The sun
3. The red sky

(Answer — 2. The sun)

Other National Symbols of Japan

The raccoon dog - Our national animal is the raccoon dog.

The 'tanuki' is a magical and friendly spirit who appears in many Japanese mythical stories. The tanuki offers blessings and good fortune to human beings. These friendly tanukis are called bake-danuki.

The red-crowned crane —My country's official, national bird is the red-crowned crane. The red-crowned crane, also called Japanese cranes, is symbolically referred to as 'tansho' which translates to a 'bird of happiness and long life.' The snow-white Japanese cranes are believed to be the largest and heaviest type in the world and are quite rare.

The Chrysanthemum Seal — The 16-petaled yellow chrysanthemum flower is a symbol of the Japanese Emperor. The chrysanthemum seal also called as 'Kikumon,' in Japanese and represents the power and authority of the Japanese emperor. You can find this seal on Japanese passports, too.

The green pheasant is also considered to be the national bird of Japan, though its status is unofficial. The green pheasant is believed to be the messenger of the sun goddess, Amaterasu. The Japanese people believe that the green pheasant detects an earthquake a few minutes before it happens, and the birds starts making loud sounds to warn people. Very useful, isn't it? This pretty, colorful bird is found all over Kyushu, Honshu, and Shikoku.

The Japanese Emperors do not have any power. But, they are still respected a lot as being part of old and important traditions and cultures of this country. (I will tell you more about the Japanese emperors later on).

The Koi — The Koi is the national fish of Japan. This special fish symbolizes wealth, good fortune, determination, and success which are important traits of the Japanese people. These colorful fish, however, find it difficult to survive because their bright colors attract predators like cats, raccoons, etc.

The koi fish is so intelligent that you can train it to eat from your hand and even ring a bell to get a treat.

Japanese Currency

The average life of a 10000¥ note is 4-5 years, and that of the lower denominations is 1-2 years. Japanese coins come in the following denominations: 1, 5, 10, 50, 100, and 500.

The weight of Japanese currency coins increases with its value. So, a 500¥ coin is heaviest. Therefore, the 1¥ coin is the lightest. The 1¥ coin is so light that it can float on a glass of water. It weighs only 1 gm. Maybe, we should try to see if this really works.

The yen is the Japanese currency. Its symbol is ¥. There are four denominations of notes: 1000¥, 2000¥, 5000¥, and 10000¥. The denomination of a note is its value.

Just to give you an idea, here are the costs of some of the common things we buy for our homes:

Milk
A liter of regular milk costs about 184¥

Bread
A 500g loaf of bread costs about 190¥

Clothes
A pair of Levis jeans cost about 6700¥

CHAPTER 2

WEATHER IN JAPAN

Japan has four clear, distinct seasons. Each season is beautiful in its own way. Here is a small breakup of the seasons in Japan:

Spring

The beautiful spring season lasts from March to May, and most visitors choose this time to come to Japan. It is not very hot and is very pleasant during this time of the year. This is the time when the iconic cherry blossoms are in full bloom, and my country is great to look at. A lot of festivals also take place during this time.

For people living in Japan, springtime is the beginning of a new school year. We wake up from the snow and cold of the winter and get ready to welcome visitors, flowers, festivals, and more.

Don't miss out on walking under the cherry blossom trees. This is also the time when the daughters of Japan are given extra attention. The Hina Matsuri (Girls' Day) is celebrated on March 3rd. You can read up more on this special day in the 'Culture and Traditions' chapter.
The Golden Week is also celebrated during springtime, and the festivities last for up 10 days right from April 29th until May 8th. Strawberry picking is another common activity you can enjoy after the Golden

Summer

Summer in Japan lasts from June to August. During summer, there is heavy rainfall, and the weather is quite hot. The rainfall and high temperatures can make Japan look like a steam bath. The best places to visit in summer are the northern parts such as the Hokkaido Island.

We are not deterred by the heat and humidity of the Japanese summer. Even during this time, fantastic fireworks are organized right through the country.

The days when the temperature in Japan goes over 30°C (86°F) are called manatsubi or midsummer days.

Those days when the temperature crosses 35°C (95°F) are called mōshobi or sweltering days.

Make sure you carry cooling sprays and sheets to keep yourself cool in summer. Of course, drink plenty of water. The folding fan is the best and the most natural way of staying cool in summer.

Parts of Kyushu and Okinawa are hit by typhoons during this time. All outdoor activities should be canceled in case there is a warning of an oncoming typhoon.

There are sudden downpours during summer, and you can never be sure when the rains will come. So, you must have clothes to protect yourself from these sudden downpours.

Autumn

The autumn season in Japan lasts from September to November. This season is also a great time to come to my country. The temperatures are not uncomfortable, and you can get to see some wonderful flowers blooming. Some southern parts of Japan tend to get hit by typhoons during autumn, and therefore, we need to plan well before traveling there.

Two Japanese words related to the fall season in Japan are momoji and koyo. Koyo is the name given to the changing colors of the leaves. Momoji is used to refer to one particular species of a maple tree which is like the Japanese standard for the changing color leaves from green to red to yellow or brown.

In Tokyo, we make it a point to visit Rikugien Garden in which large, towering trees slowly change their colors from green to red, then orange, and then gold. We normally go during sunset and watch the beautiful orange color of the setting sun mix with the orange/red/gold of the leaves. It's a beautiful sight.

In Mt. Takao, a special Autumn Leaves Festival takes place. It's just an hour's train ride from Tokyo and is perfect for a day's family picnic.

Winter

Almost the entire country is covered in snow during winter converting it into a magical land. Some parts of Japan can get hit by snowstorms and freezing winds which can be a problem. But, otherwise, winter in Japan is the time for skiing and visiting onsens or hot springs.

Hot spring in Beppu Oita, Japan

We have strict rules to be followed when visiting an onsen. We have to follow specific rules for the following activities:

• Where to change
• Where to pick up dry towels
• Where to put the wet towels
• Which water can be used for cleansing before soaking in the hot spring.

Not following these rules is considered rude and unsociable. The Japanese people consider visiting an onsen as a way of family bonding.

CHAPTER 3

HISTORY OF JAPAN

My mother always tells me the history of a country helps us better understand the people, culture, and traditions. Therefore, I will share with you important historical information about my country.

The first time people came to Japan was 30,000 years ago. At that time, the islands of Japan were connected to Korea and Siberia by land strips. So, these original settlers to Japan must have come on foot.

The first society of Japan was set up about 12,000 years, and it was called Jōmon culture. It was set up by the people who first came to Japan over 30,000 years ago. Around the time when the Jōmon culture flourished, the Ainu people came in boats from Siberia.

Cultivation of rice was introduced to the Jōmon and Ainu tribes by the Yayoi people who came to Japan around 300 B.C. The Yayoi people came from China and Korea, and they landed on Honshu Island.

The Yayoi people were skilled toolmakers, weavers, and farmers. Rice cultivation was brought to Japan by this set of people way back in 300 B.C.

Japan's earliest recorded emperor is Emperor Jimmu Tenno. According to Japanese myths, he was a descendant of the sun goddess Amaterasu and ruled over Japan from 660 B.C. until the 12th century

Just to jog your memory, Amaterasu is the sun-goddess and Tanuki (the raccoon dog) is the name given to the magical creature which appears in many Japanese myths!

The Yamato Period

This lasted from the middle of the 3rd century until 710 A.D. This is further divided into two parts; the Kofun Period (from the mid-3rd century until mid-6th century) and the Asuka Period (from the mid-6th century to around 710 A.D).

Shintoism or nature worship was the only religion practiced until the beginning of the Asuka Period. Buddhism was introduced to Japan in the Asuka Period, and it became very popular.

Most of us in Japan even today practice a religion that combines Shintoism and Buddhism. During the Asuka Period, a lot of Chinese influences also began. For example, the Chinese writing system was followed in Japan. Buddhism gained more importance than the original religion of Japan.

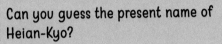

Can you guess the present name of Heian-Kyo?

1. Tokyo
2. Osaka
3. Kyoto

(Answer – 3. Kyoto)

The Nara Period

During this period, a big capital city was built, and it was designed after the Chinese capital city of that time. This new capital was built in the area which is today called Nara. The Nara Period was very slow. The capital was finally shifted to a place called Heian-Kyo in 794 which also signaled the end of the Nara Period.

The Heian Period

The Heian Period lasted from 794 until 1185. Why do you think it was called the Heian Period? Think, think! What is the name of the capital then? Yes, Heian-Kyo, and so that's why this period is called the Heian Period. At the end of the Heian Period, the real power moved from the Japanese Emperor to many powerful families and military groups. The military groups were called the shoguns and the powerful families were called daimyo. Try and remember these two names. I will test your memory sometime later.

The Feudal Period

This lasted from the end of the 12th century right until the 19th century. This was the time when the Japanese Emperors had no real power, and nearly all the power was in the hands of the daimyo and shoguns! This long period in Japanese history is further divided into smaller periods. I will tell you only the important events in each period.

The Kamakura Period — This period lasted from 1185 to 1333-35, and it is named after the city of Kamakura which was the most important power center for the shoguns who ruled at that time.

The Muromachi Period — Lasting between 1336 and 1573, the power in Japan was in the hands of the Ashikaga Shogunate (shogunate is to

Do you know that the first Europeans to set foot on Japanese soil were the Portuguese? They landed in 1542. What do you think was one of the most important elements they brought from Europe?

1. Rice
2. Guns and firearms
3. Buddhism

(Answer — 2. Guns and Firearms)

This was the first time the Japanese knew about guns and firearms! After 1542, merchants, businessmen, and missionaries from other European nations including the Netherlands, Spain, and England landed in Japan.

The Azuchi-Momoyama Period During this important time, many parts of Japan were united together and the country's military power expanded. Remember the Portuguese had brought guns and firearms to Japan?

In fact, the country military strength grew so much that one of the rulers during that time, Toyotomi Hideyoshi, wanted to conquer Korea and China! He couldn't do it, and after he died in 1598, Japan gave up this attempt.

Many Koreans migrated to Japan during this period. These people were highly skilled at pottery and other forms of art. Some were scholars, too. The Japanese learned a lot from these Koreans.

The Edo Period — During the Edo Period, a lot of developments took place in Japan. Samurais became the highest group in society. Look further down to know about these amazing Samurai warriors.

The field of art grew and expanded during the Edo Period. New types of theaters opened up. Trade flourished too during the Edo Period. The shogunate in Japan ended with the Boshin War which took place in 1868. After this, the power went back to the Japanese Emperor.

The Great Samurais of Japan

Any Japanese history lesson is incomplete without talking about the great samurai warriors. Here are some really interesting facts about these legendary warriors of Japan:

- The samurais were skilled warriors who came from noble families.
- They generally served the local lords.
- The samurais fought for their feudal lords and protected their lands, family, and everything else.
- Rice was the payment that the samurais received for their work.
- The samurais had outstanding skills in martial arts. They could fight on horseback, on the ground, armed or unarmed.
- The favorite weapon of the samurais was the sword. A samurai valued his sword so much that he even worshipped it. It was his most prized possession!

- Did you know that making a samurai sword had a long, complex process? Only specially qualified sword smiths were allowed to make them.
- Each samurai carried two types of swords: one was a long one called Katana and the other was a short one called Tanto.
- There were four classes of people in Japanese society at that time including samurais, artisans, merchants and farmers. And like I said earlier, samurais occupied the highest place in society.

The samurais followed a strict code of conduct. Do you know the name of this code of conduct?

1. Bushido
2. The Samurai Lessons
3. The Habits of the Samurai

(Answer – 1. Bushido)

The Bushido code of conduct for the samurais called for high levels of valor, self-discipline, self-sacrifice, and duty.

The Period of Seclusion

Seclusion means to keep things away or closed to outside influence. There was a period in Japan when the rulers secluded Japan from the rest of the world. The Japanese term for this seclusion is 'sakoku.' The rulers thought that the European traders, businessmen, and missionaries wanted to take control of Japan. So, they did not allow any foreigners to set foot in the country. Only the Dutch and Chinese were allowed to enter Japan. This policy started from the early 17th century and lasted for about 200 years. However, Japan continued to learn from other parts of the world even during this seclusion period.

The seclusion period ended when the Americans came with ships and modern goods to trade with Japan.

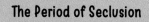

The Meiji Period

After the end of the Edo Period, the power was back in the hands of the Japanese Emperor Meiji. The feudal system ended, and a lot of Western influences were brought into Japan. The government and legal systems are copied from the US and other Western countries.

From this time until World War II, Japan fought a lot of wars with other countries including Russia, Korea, China, and more. At the end of World War I, Japan was in a very good position globally. But, at the end of World War II, Japan was in a bad state.

After World War II, the US occupied Japan and gave us a lot of help in terms of money and technology. And from then on, Japan has moved forward. I am proud to say that my country is a global leader in technology, the automobile industry, the electronics industry, and many, many other fields.

And finally, let me end this chapter with this note; the current modern period happening in Japan is called the Heisei Period. We have survived numerous earthquakes and tsunamis and have come out of each natural calamity stronger than before.

The Japanese monarchy (a form of government in which one person is the head, and he is called a monarch) is the oldest surviving one in the world. The present monarch is Emperor Akihito who is the 125th in an unbroken line of Japanese emperors.

Emperor Akihito is called 'tenno' in the Japanese language. Emporers live in the Imperial Palace in Tokyo. In the modern world, the Japanese Emperor has no real power. It is now a democracy, and the power of the government is in the hands of the Japanese Constitution and the elected democratic government representatives.

What is the name of the Japanese Parliament?
1.   The National Diet of Japan
2.   The Parliament of Japan
3.   Japan's House of Parliament

(Answer – 1. The National Diet of Japan)

One interesting point is the Japanese language does not have a clear 'R' sound. Therefore, Ronald McDonald (the famous character of McDonald's restaurants) is known as Donald McDonald in my country!

The Japanese Language

The Japanese language can be a bit complex for you initially. But, here are some really interesting facts about my country's language. There are:

* No singular and plural
* No gender forms
* No articles (a, an, or the)

There are only 48 sounds you have to learn, and therefore, speaking the Japanese language is very easy. But writing in my language can prove to be quite a challenge, and the biggest of them all is how to write the characters.

Religions in Japan

Shintoism is the ancient religion in Japan. Shinto means 'the way of the gods. Shintoism is believed to have started in 1000 B.C. but is still practiced with fervor. Shintoism teaches that spirits called 'kami' exist in this world.

Kami can be found everywhere such as in animals, rivers, stones, mountains, trees, forests, some people, and sometimes in the dead.

Each shrine has a highly sacred, innermost hall in which the kami resides. Only priests are allowed into this sacred space in the shrine.

Who do you think is the most important kami in Japan? (Hint: She is believed to be the ancestor of Japanese Emperors). It's the sun goddess, Amaterasu.

Buddhism came to Japan from China in the 6th century.
In most modern Japanese homes, both Shintoism and Buddhism are followed. For example, on New Year's Eve, Buddhist bells are rung, and on New Year's Day, people visit both Buddhist temples and Shinto shrines to pray for good fortune.

Wedding rituals are celebrated as per Buddhist traditions and funeral rituals are performed as per Shinto rites.

Purity is the most important element in Shintoism. Therefore, before entering a Shinto shrine, people have to wash their hands, rinse their mouths, and purify themselves.

A bell is rung to summon (or call) the kami and then offerings of money and rice are made. Then, we bow and clap twice to welcome the kami we have called. Then, we bow again before leaving the shrine.

You would be surprised to know that there are more than 80,000 shrines all over Japan. Every shrine celebrates an annual festival where the kami of the shrine is worshipped grandly followed by a grand feast of food and drink. During these annual festivals, the kami are carried in portable shrines and are in processions around the area.

National holidays

New Year's Day — Called ganjitsu, New Year's Day in Japan is celebrated on January 1st like most other western countries. But, the traditions in Japan are unique to our country. Visiting shrines and temples is an important event for everyone.

We treat each new year like a fresh start where we leave behind the worries of the previous year and begin the new year with happiness and joy.

The best part of this period is that all schools and almost all businesses are closed until January 3rd! People all over Japan are in a celebratory mood.

National Foundation Day

In Japanese, this day is called Kenkoku Kinen no Hi and is celebrated on February 11th each year. It commemorates the formation of the Japanese nation.

The National Flag is raised and important people give speeches. We children love to wave our national flags and show our pride for our country.

It is believed that the first Japanese Emperor ascended the throne on this day.

Hina-arare are sweet and colorful rice puffs eaten on girls day.

Girls' Festival

This is one of my favorite festivals. It is celebrated every year on March 3rd. On this day, my parents shower extra love and affection on me. In all homes, parents wish and pray for the success and happiness of their daughters.

My mother and I decorate our home with dolls and peach blossoms on this festival which is called Hina Matsuri. Nearly all homes in Japan follow this decorating tradition.

Spring Equinox – Celebrated on March 20/21, this holiday symbolizes the end of winter and the beginning of warm spring. On this day, many people visit the graves of their ancestors to honor them through offerings.

We refer to this national holiday/festival as Shunbun No Hi. It is an important and popular holiday for farmers as on this day they pray for an abundant harvest.

Osaka, Japan - April 29, 2017: crowd of people for Golden Week at entrance of Ebisu Bashi-Suji Shopping Street with its colorful neon in Namba District, one of main tourist destinations in Osaka.

The Golden Week – This is a week of festivities started from April 29th until May 8th. Nearly everyone in Japan gets off during this week. Some of the important holidays that fall during this time are:

- **Showa Day** – This is the start of the Golden Week. Emperor Showa was the 124th Emperor of Japan, and he was much loved and respected. His birthday was celebrated on April 29th each year. After Emperor Showa died in 1989, April 29th is now celebrated as Showa Day.

- **Constitutional Memorial Day** – This day falls on May 3rd every year. It was on this day in 1947 the Constitution of Japan came into effect.

- **Greenery Day** – May 4th is Midori no Hi or Greenery Day to celebrate the power and beauty of nature and the environment.

- **Children's Day** – Another favorite holiday of mine is Children's Day (Kodomo no Hi) which falls on May 5th. On this day, people pray for the health and happiness of the children of Japan.

Koinobori or "carp streamers" are flown in Japanese houses during Children's Day. There's a song that goes: "Higher than the roof-tops are the koinobori. The large carp is the father. The smaller carp are the children. They seem to be having fun swimming!"

Nature and the traditon of respect are both highly valued concepts in our culture. We even have holidays to celebrate them!

Ocean Day
This holiday falls on the third Monday in July each year. We remember and thank the oceans for its abundance to the Japanese people. After all, we are an island nation, and the ocean and sea play a very important part of our lives.

Mountain Day
Again, mountains are an important aspect of Japan, and August 11 every year is set aside to worship and thank mountains. Remember that nature worship is a crucial part of Shintoism? We believe spirits called kami live in all natural things.

The Elderly Day
The Japanese people treat all the elders with a lot of respect, and a special day is kept aside to give thanks and appreciate the elderly for their work in the community. Called Keiro no Hi in the Japanese language, this important holiday falls on the third Monday in September.

Thanksgiving Day
In Japan, Thanksgiving (called Kinro Kansha no Hi) is celebrated to thank the workers of Japan. It falls on November 23rd and is also referred to as Labor Day.

The Emperor's Birthday
As you already know, the present person on the Chrysanthemum Throne (yes, the name given to the Japanese throne) is Emperor Akihito. His birthday falls on December 23rd which is a national holiday.

Health and Sports Day
This day falls on the second Monday in October every year. This national holiday is to commemorate the opening ceremony of the 1964 Tokyo Olympics. On this day, people are reminded of the importance of health and sports for an active life.

Popular/ Favorite Foods

Can you name the staple food of Japan? (Hint: it was introduced to Japan way back in the 3rd century). Yes! You are right. Rice, it is!

While on the subject of food, what is the most commonly used cutlery in Japan?
1.   Forks and spoons
2.   Hand
3.   Chopsticks

(Answer – 3. Chopsticks)

Nearly 24 billion pairs of chopsticks are used in Japan each year. Phew!

Bento box – This is the traditional kids' lunch boxes that are filled with sushi and other goodies and treats to take to school.

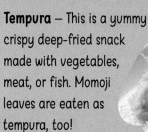

Sushi – raw fish rolled in rice; initially, you might find it strange to eat raw fish. But the seasonings and the fish itself can be quite delicious after trying it for a couple of times.

Ramen – Egg noodles in a soupy broth; Soba is the buckwheat variety of Ramen. It is important to slurp noodles in Japan because slurping is a way of telling the cook that the dish is delicious.

Tempura – This is a yummy crispy deep-fried snack made with vegetables, meat, or fish. Momoji leaves are eaten as tempura, too!

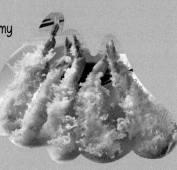

Yakitori – Cubes of chicken on skewers eaten with a dip of salty soy sauce. Yakiton are pork cubes version of yakitori.

Taiyaki – Shaped like a fish, taiyaki is a sweet dish with delicious fillings.

The Japanese People

The Japanese people are known for their highly disciplined way of life, politeness, and hard work. The trains in Japan are the most punctual in the entire world. The average delay is just 18 seconds!

We are also fun-loving people. Let me tell you more about our culture.

Precision and perfection are very important elements for the Japanese people. Farmers grow square watermelons so that they can stack them perfectly!

The importance of the Japanese bow - Greeting is a formal ritual in my country. Do you know how we greet people? We bow, sometimes with folded hands, and sometimes with our hands on the side. We bow:

• To say hello or goodbye

• Before starting and after ending a meeting or a get-together

• When we thank someone

• When we say we are sorry

• When we congratulate someone

• When requesting someone for a favor or help

• When we worship

Also, there are rules to how low the bow should be. We take our bowing ritual very seriously. However, handshakes are also used to greet people in modern society, especially when we meet foreigners.

Social Etiquettes

Japan has a hierarchy system which describes how people are ranked in order of importance. Therefore, the social hierarchy would mean how people are ranked in society.

In Japan, we are very conscious of peoples' ages and statuses in society. Elders get the most respect. Kids like us are taught to treat all elders with unconditional respect. Therefore, when we kids bow to grandparents, we bow really low.

The Japanese people are very strict about such social rules because harmony and peace are important to us. We believe that politeness, working together, and personal responsibility at each level bring about harmony! Ok, that's enough of serious stuff!

Do you know how I refer to older students, or seniors, in school? As 'senpai.' The seniors refer to us as 'kohai.' Using informal language with seniors is considered rude in Japan. Also, in every group, the eldest member gets the highest respect.

It's also worth menioning that tipping is not allowed in Japan. People feel insulted when they are tipped. So, when you visit a restaurant, remember NOT to tip.

When entering a home, we remove our footwear first. Nearly all homes have raised floors by the doorway to indicate the point where footwears must be removed. Every house will have home slippers for you to wear inside. Also, if a house has a tatami mat room, even home slippers have to be removed. And, if you are using the restroom, there are separate bathroom slippers for that too!

You cannot blow your nose in public because it is considered rude. Find a restroom, and blow your nose there.

Akihabara is recognized as the center of Japanese "otaku culture" (pop culture obsession) and has tons of shops dedicated to anime, manga, videogames, and electronics!

Stock photo ID:1134889165

Giant robot statue from the anime "Gundam" in Odaiba Leisure District

You cannot come to Japan and not talk about the most favorite things for kids: cartoons, toys, video games, and comics! We have a rich history of manga and anime in Japan. Just to clarify things a bit, anime refers to animation while manga refers to comics and cartoons.

An interesting point here is many Japanese animation movies are inspired from manga. So, for us kids, everything is connected!

Fun fact: More paper gets used for making manga than toilet paper in my country!

Ra-awr!

Anime and manga are so popular in Japan that we have made the famed Godzilla an official citizen of Japan!

33

I have already told you how important nature, plants, and animals are to the Japanese culture. We believe that kami, or spirits, live everywhere in nature so we take great care of our environment, forests, trees, and wildlife! Let me tell you about some of the most common plants and animals found in Japan.

Japan stretches in the form of an arc from north to south. The climate in the north of the country is very different from the south of Japan. In southern Japan, you see a lot of evergreen trees with broad leaves such as evergreen oaks and chinquapins.

In the north of Japan, especially in Hokkaido, coniferous trees like Sakhalin fir and Yeddo spruce can be seen. Another name for evergreen trees is coniferous which means they keep their leaves right through the year. They don't shed their leaves.

Japan has four seasons and different flowers bloom throughout the year.

Plum Blossoms - In early spring, you will see plum blossoms blooming. When we see plum blossoms blooming, we know that winter is nearing its end. The plum tree holds a lot of significance in Japanese culture. It stands for hope and vitality and is a sign that tells people to keep hope because warm, cozy weather is not far away.

Cherry Blossoms – These flowers are an important icon of Japan as they are our national flower. They bloom in mid-spring.

Do you know the Japanese name for cherry blossoms?
1. Sakura
2. Ume
3. Kiku

Answer: Sakura!

Having a picnic under cherry blossom trees is a Japanese tradition, called 'hanami,' which is Japanese for 'flower viewing.' Such late-night picnics are called 'yozakura.' My family and I do this every year where we, along with many others in my locality, hang paper lanterns on cherry blossom trees.

Hydrangeas – Ajisai is Japanese for hydrangeas, and they bloom in the rainy season. These stunning flowers are believed to have originated in the mountains of Japan and are native to my country. These flowers are beautiful to look at. But, they are mildly poisonous. So, you have to be very careful.

Morning Glory – These gorgeous flowers bloom in midsummer. In addition to its beauty, the oil from the seeds of the morning glory is used as herbal medicine. This plant was brought to Japan by the Chinese during the Nara Period. (You can reread the section about the Nara Period in the chapter 'The History of Japan.') In many Japanese houses, morning glory is grown as a 'heat curtain' to keep out the heat of the summer.

Chrysanthemums – These flowers, called kiku in Japanese, bloom in autumn (or as the Americans call it, fall). You can imagine the importance of these flowers as the Imperial Seal is made after the chrysanthemum (remember the Chrysanthemum Seal – the 16-petaled flower).

The chrysanthemum was brought to my country way back in 400 AD by Buddhist monks from China. The Japanese Emperors loved these flowers so much that they were inspired to create the Chrysanthemun Throne.

Other common plants that you will find in many gardens and streets of Japan include maples, camellias, daphnes, gingkos, and magnolias. Japanese people love flowers, plants, and trees.

Native Animals of Japan

Japan is home to over 160 varieties of wild mammals and numerous types of insects and birds. Here are some animals that are unique to Japan:

Japanese serow — This is a species of deer that is found only in Japan. The Japanese name for this deer is 'kamoshika'. These unique and beautiful animals are slow creatures. They are also very secretive animals who keep to themselves.

Iriomote wildcat — These cats are found on the Iriomote Island which is located in the southernmost part in Japan. Both the male and female Iriomote cats meow and howl like domestic cats.

This cat is a great swimmer and is related to the leopard. This animal has been declared as one of the country's national treasures, and the government has many laws to protect these animals from becoming extinct.

Extinct means to 'disappear from the earth altogether and forever.' For example, dinosaurs are an extinct species of animals.

Amami hare — Amami hares (or rabbits) are found on two small islands Amami Ōshima and Tokunoshima, which are part of the Ryuku Archipelago in the southern part of Japan.

> **Do you know what an archipelago is?**
> 1. A group of mountains
> 2. A group of islands
> 3. A group of rivers
>
> (Answer — 2. A group of islands)

The Amami hare eats only plant food such as nuts, leaves, berries, etc. These small animals are eaten by cats, dogs, snakes, mongoose, etc. These animals are also protected by the Japanese government as they are considered endangered species, which means in danger of becoming extinct.

Giant flying squirrel — Found both in China and Japan, the male giant flying squirrel is called buck, and the female is called doe (yes, like the deer).

You can find them in evergreen forests on Honshu, Kyushu, and Shikoku islands. Did you know that flying squirrels have a web of skin (like the duck's webbed foot) between their legs that helps them to fly and glide among the trees?

Japanese black bear

You can see these black bears on Honshu, Kyushu, and Shikoku islands. During most of the winters, the Japanese black bears hibernate (sleep in their dens for extended periods of time).

These animals are excellent tree climbers. They have two kinds of homes; one home is their den in the hollows of trees, under the ground, or under huge rocks. They also build nests (called enza in Japanese) on trees for eating and resting.

Other animals and birds native to Japan include the Japanese macaque, wild boar, Ezo brown bear, sable, striped squirrel, Sakhalin red fox, bush warbler, swallow, common pheasant, copper pheasant, and many more.

The oceans and seas around Japan are also home to multiple aquatic plants and animals. Japan is a rich, diverse nation when it comes to its plant and animal life.
And finally, the swan flies from its home in Siberia to spend winters in northern Japan.

CHAPTER 6

FAMOUS PEOPLE FROM JAPAN

Many Japanese people have achieved world fame through their various activities. I feel proud to tell you about a few of them.

During his time, Musashi inspired a lot of fictional stories about his life. Even now, he is still referenced a lot in samurai novels, video games, and manga!

Haruki Murakami — Born in 1949, Haruki Murakami is a very famous writer and novelist. He has won multiple awards for his works. He was first inspired to write a novel when he was watching a baseball game. He said this himself in an interview and in his memoir "What I Talk About when I talk About Running"

Murakami's books have been translated into 50 languages and have sold millions of copies outside Japan!

Miyamoto Musashi — He is one of the most famous and popular samurais in Japan. He is believed to have lived between 1584 and 1645. He became renowned through stories of his unique double-bladed swordsmanship and undefeated record in his 61 duels!

In addition to being a master swordsman, Musashi was also a great writer, philosopher, teacher, sculptor, painter and calligrapher!

Do you know the name of the book he wrote that is used by management schools even today?

1. The Sword Book
2. How to Win a Sword Fight
3. The Book of Five Rings

Answer: (3) The Book of Five Rings

Akira Kurosawa — He was born on March 23rd, 1910, and even after his death, he is one of the most respected film directors of all times. Did you know that he made 30 movies in 50 years?

Rashomon was his first movie that gained worldwide popularity. This movie made the Westerners want to watch other Japanese movies, too. He was the given the Academy Award for Lifetime Achievement in 1990. Just to jog your memory, Academy Awards are more commonly known as the Oscars. Many of his movies were remade in other languages. One of his most popular movies, The Seven Samurai, was made in 1954 and has been remade multiple times.

Yoko Ono — Married to the famous Beatles singer, John Lennon, Yoko Ono is a woman who fights against wars and preaches the importance of world peace. She started learning music from the age of 4.

Yoko Ono and her famous husband, John Lennon, used every opportunity to spread the message of world peace. They staged protests against the Vietnam War that was happening when they got married in 1969.

Did you know that Yoko Ono in Japanese means 'Ocean Child?'

Akira Toriyama — He was born on April 5th, 1955, and is a manga artist and illustrator. His first brush with manga was when he won an amateur manga competition.

If you cannot recall his name, just think of Dragon Ball Z. Well, this highly popular cartoon character whose stories have been seen by three generations was created by Akira Toriyama. His other equally popular works include Dr. Slump, Dragon Quest, Chrono Trigger, and Blue Dragon.

He is a very shy person and does not give interviews to journalists or even allow his photographs to be taken. But, the Japanese people are very proud of him.

Momofuku Ando — He was inspired to create instant noodles when there was a big food shortage in Japan after World War II. After surrendering to the US, the Japanese government encouraged everyone to eat bread instead of noodles because noodle companies were having a difficult time surviving, and there was a short supply of this favorite Japanese food. He sold his packet of Chicken Ramen in 1958. After the Americans started consuming noodles, he started the now-famous noodles in a cup which requires you to simply add hot water.

Today, there are two museums in Japan in honor of Momofuku Ando; one in Ikeda in Osaka and another one in Yokohama, Tokyo.

Large and Popular Companies of Japan

Toyota – Toyota which is now a famous car company started off as a textile business. Even today, Toyota has a textile division. Can you guess who is the founder of Toyota?

1. Kiichiro Toyoda
2. Akira Toyota
3. Hirohito Toyota

(Answer – 1. Kiichiro Toyoda; yes the founder spells his name differently from his company's name)

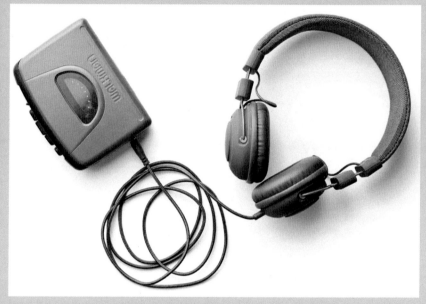

Honda – The Honda Company was started in 1946 by ex-racing driver Soichiro Honda who was also an engineer. The Honda Motor Company was started as the Honda Technical Research Institute. The company started with motorcycles and motorized bikes before moving to cars.

Sony – Sony Corporation is a world-famous gadget giant. Your PlayStation is a product of this giant electronics company. You can ask your parents (or grandparents) and they will tell you lots of stories about the famous Sony Walkman. Sony entered the world of electronics with a rice cooker.

Nintendo — Think of video games, and the first name that pops in your head is Nintendo, right?

Can you name one of the first, and perhaps the most popular video game character developed by this famous company?

1. Zelda
2. Mario
3. Pikachu

(Answer – 2, Mario)

Fun Fact: Nintendo started off as a playing card company and eventually ventured into video games with their release of home consoles and arcade machines.

Canon — The first name of Canon was Precision Optical Industry Co. Ltd. It developed the first camera, and called it the Kwannon, the name of the Buddhist Goddess of Mercy. The Kwannon was simplified into Canon. Kwannon was the first logo of the company.

She is believed to have 11 faces and 1000 hands! But, in the company's logo, the Goddess has 16 arms and sits on a lotus. Of course, today, this logo is also simplified into a cool and modern one. Canon today manufactures office equipment such as printers, scanners, and copiers, along with cameras.

As you already know, Tokyo is the capital of Japan. Other major cities include Osaka, Kyoto, Nagoya, and Sapporo. Let me give you a peek into each of these cities.

Tokyo

Here are some of the top interesting facts of Tokyo:

• It is the largest city in the world in terms of population and size. The number of people living in Tokyo is over 38 million, and the area of this city covers 8500 sq.km. (about 3280 square miles).

The cherry blossom festival in Tokyo has been going on for centuries. One of the most popular places to enjoy the cherry blossom festival is Nagoya Castle.

• There is a huge variety of vending machines in Tokyo that sell everything from clothes to food to toys, and more.

• The Tokyo Skytree stands at 634 meters (about 2080 ft) and is the tallest building in the world. The observation tower gives an amazing view of Tokyo. Don't miss this while here. Of course, you cannot go alone. Your parents or some responsible elder must accompany you.

• Harajuku Fashion is a famous Japanese teenager fashion style that is popular all over the world.

Tskuji Market — This is a huge fish market where you can see an amazing variety of fish and seafood being sold and bought.

Tokyo Disneyland — A must-see for kids, this place gives you a complete Disney feel. There is no way any kid will come away from Tokyo Disneyland disappointed or unhappy. I think the only reason a child will be unhappy in this amazing place is when it is time to leave!

The Fire Museum — Here, you can dress up like a fireman and play in helicopters and fire trucks.

National Museum of Nature and Science — It is the best science museum in Tokyo, and you have a wide variety of hands-on experiments you can try for yourself. There are kid-friendly exhibits on every floor.

Ueno Zoo — You can see a wide variety of animals including tigers, elephants, pandas, and more.

Osaka

Osaka is another important Japanese city located close to Kyoto, the old capital of Japan. Did you know that Osaka is called the Manchester of Japan? It got its name because of its flourishing textile industry. The word Osaka means a 'large slope' or a 'large hill'.

Osaka is called the 'nation's kitchen' because it was the center of rice trading from the time of the Edo Period. Today, it is a foodie paradise.

Okonomiyaki is a Kansai dish often called Japanese pancake or pizza.

Can you name one of the most famous dish in Osaka?

1. Sushi
2. Bento box
3. Okonomiyaki

Answer
3 - Okonomiyaki

The Osaka Castle — You can learn a lot more about Japanese history, the samurai clans, and enjoy the wide open spaces. This castle was built, destroyed, and rebuilt many times since 1583 when its construction first started.

The present structure was built in 1931 and miraculously survived air raids during World War II. You can see beautiful gardens, gates, turrets, moats, huge stone walls, and more.

Universal Studios — The first Universal Studio outside the US was opened in Osaka. You can see all the effects of Hollywood here including Harry Potter and his Wizarding World, Jurassic Park, Despicable Me, and more. I have visited Universal Studios twice with my parents, and they were even more excited with each trip than I was.

Osaka Aquarium — This place has 8 levels with 15 huge tanks holding a wide variety of sea creatures and fish. Also, there are exhibits showing you the forests of Japan, the Great Barrier Reef, the Pacific Ocean, and more. You should set aside 3 hours to see everything there is to see in the Osaka Aquarium.

Tennoji Zoo — The Tennoji Zoo is slightly smaller zoo than many others in Japan. There are only 1000 animals. But, it is a wonderful place to walk around and meet your favorite 4-legged animals. There is a lake with turtles, too. If you want to break from animals, you can enjoy yourself on the playgrounds within the zoo.

Other places in Osaka that are worth visiting are Legoland Discovery Center, Kids Plaza & Omigachi Park, Animal Cafes, Nakanoshima Park, and more.

Kyoto

As you already know, Kyoto was the old capital of Japan for over 1000 years, for this reason, Kyoto is called the thousand-year capital. The capital shift to Tokyo Around 1868 and happened over a period of time.

Some of the must-see places in Kyoto for us kids are:

Kiyomizu-dera Temple — This temple is a UNESCO World Heritage Site and is situated in a hilly, wooded area in the eastern part of Kyoto. The meaning of Kiyomizu-dera is 'Pure Water Temple.' It was built in 780 A.D. on the site of the Otowa Waterfall and is one of the most revered Buddhist temples in Japan.

UNESCO is a global organization that keeps track of and preserves the ancient and beautiful monuments all over the world. The full name of UNESCO is The United Nations Educational, Scientific, and Cultural Organization and is part of the United Nations.

The three most famous festivals in Kyoto include:

• **Aoi-Matsuri** - This takes place at the start of summer.

• **Gion-Matsuri** - This festival happens in midsummer

• **idai-Matsuri** - This is the autumn festival in Kyoto.

People come from all over the world to participate in these festivals.

Fushimi Inari Shrine

This Shinto shrine is known for the thousands of torii gates that run up the mountain. Torii is a special gate at the beginning of every Shinto shrine.

The Fushimi Inari Shrine is dedicated to the god of rice, or Inari. Visiting this temple means a hike up the mountain.

Sapporo

Sapporo is the capital of Hokkaido, one of the four main islands of Japan which is located in the north. There is a famous snow festival that takes place every year here. Here are some of the best places to visit in Sapporo:

Takino Suzuran Hillside National Park — Kids are taught about the importance of environmental protection through the use of interactive toys and equipment. You can take guided tours through the forests.

One of my favorite is Sapporo Satoland — You can make sausages and butter in this agricultural theme park in Sapporo. You can harvest vegetables, play with farm animals, and more. In the winter, this entire place gets converted into a snow-covered playground.

Okurayama Viewing Point – After catching the stunning views offered in this place, you can ski jump down the steep slope. This place was used for sporting events in the 1972 Winter Olympics Games.

Moerenuma Park – This park was created by Isamu Noguchi, a sculptor. It is built on a place that was a waste disposal center earlier and is called 'landscape sculpture' as it allows you to experience the four seasons of Japan in one place.

Sapporo Maruyama Zoo – The facilities for the large number of animals living here are built to recreate their natural habitats. The zoo keepers believe that the animals will show their natural instincts in such situations.

Sunpiazza Aquarium – Located close to a big shopping center in the heart of the city, Sunpiazza Aquarium holds a wide variety of sea creatures brought from the neighboring seas as well as the southern oceans. There is a 'touch pool' where you can touch starfish and crabs.

Conclusion

So, now that we have come to the end of the journey of Japan, take a few minutes to answer the following questions so I know how much you enjoyed your trip to my country.

What excited you the most in this trip across Japan?

Which was your favorite city and why?

If you do come back to Japan again, which is the one place you will not want to miss, and why?

Remember I had asked you to memorize these two names, and I will test you!

I hope you enjoyed the things I showed and told you about my country. I enjoyed myself thoroughly. I thought it would be a great idea to finish our trip across Japan with an easy quiz. So, here goes:

What is the name used to refer to the powerful families of the Feudal Period in Japan?
1. Daimyo
2. Dante
3. Descartes

(Answer – 1. Daimyo; the other two people have no connection with Japan!)

During the feudal period, there were powerful military groups as well. What were they called?
1. The Shanghai Warriors
2 The Japanese Commanders
3 The shoguns

(Answer – 3. The shoguns)

What is the name of the special lunch box in Japan?
1. Bento box
2. The food box
3. The lunch box

(Answer – 1. Bento box)

What are the top two religions followed in Japan?
1. Protestant and Catholic
2. Hinduism and Buddhism
3. Shintoism and Buddhism

(Answer – 3. Shintoism and Buddhism)

How long have people been living in Japan?
1. Since the 1500s
2. For over 30,000 years
3. For over 10,000 years

(Answer – 3. For over 30,000 years)

What are the main land formations that make up Japan?
1. It consists of four main islands and over 4000 smaller islands
2. It is a peninsula
3. It is one large island

(Answer – 1. It consists of four main islands and over 4000)

What are the monarchs of Japan called?
1. Shoguns
2. Daimyo
3. Emperors

(Answer – 3. Emperors)

I have thoroughly enjoyed this journey through Japan with you. I hope you come back and with more friends next time!

What is the most important and common form of greeting in Japan?
1. A handshake
2. A hug
3. A bow

(Answer – 3. A bow)

What shape will you find in the center of the Japanese flag?
1. A square
2. A circle
3. A triangle

(Answer – 2. A circle)

What is the nickname of Japan?
1. The Land of the Great Frontier
2. The Land of Pearls
3. The Land of the Rising Sun

(Answer – 3. The Land of the Rising Sun)

What is the currency of Japan?
1. Dollar
2. Pound
3. Yen

(Answer – 3. Yen)

I have thoroughly enjoyed this journey through France with you.
Feel free to visit us at www.dinobibi.com and check out our other titles!

Dinobibi Travel for Kids

Dinobibi History for Kids

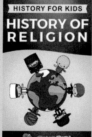
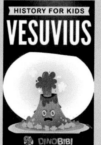

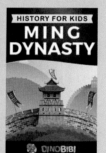

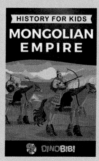